Sprouts

& SPROUTING

Sprouts

& SPROUTING

THE COMPLETE GUIDE WITH SEVENTY HEALTHY AND CREATIVE RECIPES

VALÉRIE CUPILLARD

Photography by Philippe Barret and Myriam Gauthier-Moreau

GRUB STREET | LONDON

Published in 2007 by
Grub Street
4 Rainham Close
London
SW11 6SS
Email: food@grubstreet.co.uk
Web: www.grubstreet.co.uk

First published in France by Éditions La Plage as *Graines germées*
Translation in to English by Tamsin Black

A CIP catalogue for this book is available from the British Library

10 digit ISBN 1-904943-90-X
13 digit ISBN 978-1-904943-90-7
EAN 9781904943907

Printed and bound in India

AUTHOR'S NOTE

To avoid weighing the ingredients, I have often used glasses and bowls. Here are the conversions for these
measures with American cups:
1 glass = 150 ml = 2/3 cup
1/2 glass = 75 ml = 1/3 cup
1 bowl = 500 ml = 2 cups
1 teaspoon = 5 ml = 1 teaspoon
1 tablespoon = 10 ml = 2 teaspoons

Another useful conversion: 1 soya yogurt = 120 g

Thanks to Jars Céramistes, in Anneyron in the Drôme, which lent us the crockery for the photos on pages:
3-4,13, 28-29, 31, 45, 55, 57, 61, 63, 69, 71, 73, 83, 87, 91, 93, 105,109,115, 117 and the book jacket

Preface

Sprouts are ingredients that contribute to living nutrition. Introducing sprouts, grass juices, algae, oilseeds and fresh, raw, organically grown fruit and vegetables to your diet is one of the best ways of bringing the body an excellent source of energy.

Rich in amino acids, as well as vitamins, sprouts are also recognized for their high levels of fibre and enzymes and for being antioxidants and alkaline.

A serving of sprouts with a meal will breathe fresh life into your daily eating. They will make your mealtimes fun and at the same time promote a balanced diet.

Sprouts and their shoots appeal to one's decorative instincts and are a feast for the eyes but the texture is often novel and surprising to the palate.

Unlike cooked food, eating living food is something you 'feel'. Smaller quantities generally satisfy the appetite because of the high nutritional value of sprouted seeds.

As you become experienced and familiar with this superior nutrition, you will start to become aware of the times when you need it, either in small doses or as a proper detox diet. Subtly, sprouts help us to listen to our bodies and know our requirements. Sprouts contain the power of springtime and are bursting with energy, new life and 'germination'. All of which suggests, logically enough, that they will 'kick start' the body. This is why the spring and early summer (the seasons when they grow most easily at home in the kitchen), as well as breakfast time (as an extra boost at the start of the day) are often good times to eat them.

I enjoyed getting to know all about sprouted seeds and devising recipes that would best bring out their flavour. I hope you have as much fun as I had!

VALÉRIE CUPILLARD

Contents

Sprouts and health

Germination transforms the seed and triggers a series of positive changes: the enzymes start to pre-digest, the starch is broken down into components that are simpler to digest and the level of vitamins goes up. After sprouting, the nutritional value of the seeds increases tenfold and brings the body vitamins and minerals that can be considered as bio-available.

WHAT DO WE FIND IN SPROUTED SEEDS?

Vegetable protein In green soya (mung beans), sunflower, sesame, alfalfa and broccoli sprouts, for example.

More iron Especially in fenugreek, lentils, cress, spinach, fennel, sesame, red lentils, broccoli and quinoa, etc.

Magnesium In wheat, lentils, flax, spinach, buckwheat, sunflower and sesame, etc.

Calcium In red lentils, adzuki, cress, spinach, quinoa, sesame, etc.

B-group vitamins In wheat, spinach, rice, lentils, etc.

Essential fatty acids In sunflower and sesame seed sprouts, etc.

Phosphorus, potassium, copper Present particularly in broccoli, carrots, cabbage, fennel, fenugreek, leeks, spinach and wheat.

Antioxidants Especially in alfalfa, broccoli and wheat.

Rich in vitamin C In all sprouts and particularly in alfalfa, broccoli, cress, lentils, red cabbage, and rocket.

Sprouts also have a highly alkalising effect. Eating sprouted grains and legumes can help maintain or re-establish an acid-alkaline balance.

Sprouts also have a highly alkalising effect. Eating sprouted grains and legumes can help maintain or re-establish an acid-alkaline balance. Sprouts are positively bursting with nutritional value.

9

Sprouts or shoots?

Some sprouts can be eaten as soon as they germinate, for others you need to wait for the first leaves to appear. It's a question of optimising the germination period for each seed.

Initially, a seed that has been watered and sprayed grows a shoot, which is rich with the seed's energy. The shoot develops in the dark. It is white and can be eaten in this form.

If left to grow, the sprouted seed changes and develops chlorophyll when exposed to the light. Little leaves appear together with a small shoot.

This is generally the furthest stage of development of the seed in these 'soil-less' conditions of growth. If you wait too long, the sprouted seed will wither.

Generally, grains (wheat, spelt, buckwheat, etc), oil-seeds (sesame, sunflower, pumpkin, squash, etc) and legumes (chick peas, lentils, etc) can be eaten when the sprout is about 0.5 cm, whereas the vegetable or herb seeds (fennel, radish, leeks, carrots, alfalfa, cress, parsley, coriander, dill, mustard, and so on) are eaten as leafy sprouted seeds, i.e., as delicate little green shoots of about 3 cm high.

Some seeds can be eaten throughout their development, from sprout to leafy shoot. Sunflower seeds are an example and can be eaten in the earliest stages as a sprout or, if you want higher levels of chlorophyll, as young shoots.

Some grains, like wheat or barley, can properly be grown on soil to harvest the grass (rich in chlorophyll) before putting them through a special extractor to collect the juice and remove the fibres, which are incompatible with our digestive system.

Sprouts and shoots can now be found ready packaged in the chilled section of health food aisles. The array of sprouted seeds on offer is an excellent way to try out several seeds, as all of them are very different. Everyone will have their own favourites, but you may like to start with alfalfa, which is light and delicate with a subtle flavour, as well as sunflower seed shoots for their crisp freshness.

Make sure that packaged sprouts are absolutely fresh with clear, healthy colours. If the chill chain has been broken and they have been subjected to a damp, unventilated environment, they can develop an unpleasant smell. You will soon see that if the sprouts are wilting and soft, they have no appeal. There is a broad range of packaged sprouts on offer, and it is great to be able to try so many flavours so easily: radish, onion, fennel, fenugreek, sunflower, lentil, broccoli, red cabbage, wheat, mung beans (soya), alfalfa, and so on.

Wheat juice or barley juice

In conditions other than a jar or germinator for sprouting seeds and shoots, some grains, like wheat, barley, spelt or kamut, can be grown until they become 'grass'. On contact with water, air and light (sun), grain seed turns into grass, which does not have the same components; wheat grass, for instance, does not contain gluten.

These grasses are only consumed as a juice, as this is the most suitable way for our digestive system. Otherwise they are too fibrous, so you need a special appliance to crush the grass without damaging it. It is essential, for example, to avoid any source of heat to extract the juice.

Rich in oxygen and especially chlorophyll, grass juices also have the advantage of being alkaline.

WHEAT GRASS JUICE

It takes a certain amount of organisation as well as space to grow wheat grass at home (although a balcony can be enough) and spread out the seedlings in trays of compost or soil.

Cut the wheat grass when it is 15 to 20 cm high and put it through the juicer to collect the precious, chlorophyll-rich juice.

Fresh wheat juice can be consumed as soon as it is made and in small quantities. It can be used as a detox diet or as a natural, nutritional complement to your everyday diet at certain times of life. The benefits of wheat grass juice detox diets are many and people who have tried them look on the juice as a magic potion with the power to rejuvenate! Note that wheat grass is made up of about 70 % chlorophyll, vitamins (including pro-vitamin A and vitamins B and C), eight essential amino acids, minerals and trace elements.

Wheat grass juice is consumed immediately after extraction. If you don't want to grow your own wheat grass, you will still be able to try it, as some health food restaurants and juice bars now include these green cocktails on the drinks list.

BARLEY GRASS JUICE

Barley grass can be grown in the same way as wheat grass in trays of soil or compost placed on a balcony or in the garden. Cut it when it reaches 8 to 10 cm high and put it through a juicer to collect the juice with the fibres eliminated, as these are liable to irritate the digestive system.

If you don't want to grow barley grass, the alternative is to use powdered barley grass juice. You can then reconstitute the grass juice as a detox diet or as a nutritional complement to your everyday diet at certain times of the year or of life. Of special interest in this drink is the synergy between all the constituents, making it one of the most complete health cocktails.

Uses of barley grass juice

Barley grass juice comes as a powder and is readily available in health food shops. This is what I used in the recipes on pages 114 to 117. In its instant form, it is user-friendly and often suitable to the constraints of one's timetable.

In the kitchen, you can mix it into cold sauces after dissolving the powder in a little water. It can make healthy-looking dressings that are ideal as accompaniments to springtime dishes.

Sprouting seeds at home

If you are passionate about the flavour of sprouted seeds, you will have no trouble taking the next step and starting to grow them yourself. The process can be enjoyed by young and old. Again, alfalfa seeds are good for beginners because they grow very easily, as do sunflower seeds and lentils.

• Buy seeds for sprouting that are guaranteed organic, and to begin as simply as possible, use a glass jam jar. Make sure the jar is big enough, as the seeds will bulk out once they start to germinate. In general, 2 or 3 level tablespoons of seeds in a jar is ample. Prepare several jars of seeds for sprouting one jar per day to stagger your harvests.

• Throw away any seeds you think are damaged, place those you have selected in the glass jar and cover with plenty of water. Put a piece of very fine cotton muslin (gauze or tulle, for instance) over the jar and secure with an elastic band. If the seeds are small, this will be very useful for easy rinsing and draining. If the seeds are bigger (sunflower, chickpea, etc), a sieve is just as good. Use filtered or bottled spring water for soaking and watering the little seeds.

• Leave over night.

The over-night soaking time varies according to the size of the seeds. Alfalfa, radish and some other seeds only need 3 to 4 hours, whereas chickpea, mung bean and soya seeds, for example, will need more than 10 hours.

When growing varieties of seeds of differing size, you should germinate them separately, as they will take different times to sprout.

REMINDER

- Healthy, organic seeds with no blemishes
- Soak in spring or purified water
- Rinse carefully
- Germinate in a moist environment
- Room temperature of 18° to 22°C.
- A little light but not direct sunlight

• Next day, rinse carefully through the muslin several times using spring or filtered water.

• Drain the seeds and leave them in their jar with just a film of water. Their environment needs only to be moist. Place the jar at a slight angle to stop the water stagnating and allow the air to circulate.

• Rinse the seeds at least twice a day, morning and evening, and more often if it is hot and you think the jar is drying out. The seeds should always be kept moist without being saturated. It is also important to keep them in a protected environment, hence the muslin or a lid pierced with little holes.

• For big seeds, like sunflower, pumpkin or lentil, for example, it is better to spread them out on a plate after soaking, placing a glass lid over them to keep them moist but let in the light. The seeds will then have more room to grow, the ideal being to use a 'radish' plate (a plate with holes in it on a flat plate underneath).

• Germination time varies depending on how hard the seed is: between the appearance of the small sprout and the first tiny leaves of the shoots, there can be 2 to 6 days. The ideal temperature is about 20°C. It is not necessary to put the seedlings in the light for germination to start, but once they reach the stage of small shoots, you should place the jars in a well-lit spot away from direct sunlight for the sprouts to develop chlorophyll.

• Sprouted seeds should be eaten quickly. You can stop them growing by putting them in the fridge, making sure they are not in a damp, unventilated environment where they will stagnate.

• When you change the water keeping them moist, rinse them to remove the seeds' husks (alfalfa, lentils, sunflower, etc) which tend to go black. The process is straightforward but you need to take care when rinsing that you don't damage the shoots.

HOW TO KEEP SEEDS THAT YOU WANT TO GERMINATE

Seal the bags or put them in jars and keep them in the dark. I usually keep seeds in the fridge, so that when I take them out and bring them into contact with a moist atmosphere, they are quick to revive. Organic seeds are untreated, so if you keep them in a cupboard, watch out for mites in summer!

Ideally, for small seeds, you should, of course, aim to produce them at staggered intervals in limited quantities (don't grow too many at once). This way, you will always have a fresh supply to hand.

CAN THE SEEDS BE KEPT ONCE THEY HAVE SPROUTED?

Once the sprouts are ready to be consumed, you can stop them growing by putting them in the fridge. Leave them in a slightly moist and ventilated jar (a lid with holes in it) and continue to rinse them in spring water every other day. I noticed that they kept better if they were well drained and I had dried them off a bit by putting them in a salad spinner (for less delicate shoots!). In this way they can be kept for an average of 5 days depending on the varieties.

If you decide to buy ready sprouted seeds in a packet from the chilled aisle, trust your instinct as far as keeping them goes. The shoots should sparkle with 'vitality', they must look inviting, tempting and smell fresh.

Eating sprouts

Always raw to preserve and enjoy all their benefits.

Two exceptions: some sprouts are best eaten after being briefly steamed or boiled to eliminate certain indigestible elements in them. This applies to green lentil and chick pea sprouts. They are better assimilated when prepared in this way.

WHICH TO CHOOSE

Alfalfa, red cabbage, broccoli, fenugreek, fennel, radish and mustard seeds produce fine, tender shoots. Ideal as an accompaniment to salads.

Sunflower, red lentil, whole sesame and pumpkin are seeds that can be eaten as soon as a sprout appears. They are all tender and can be eaten plain or sprinkled on all sorts of dishes.

The seeds of green lentils, mung beans (called soya beans) and adzuki, on the other hand, grow bigger shoots. They are the only ones that lend themselves to a brief cook in a wok, for example.

To give your recipes an Asian flavour, soya sprouts or sunflower seed shoots can be briefly sautéed.

For practical use that is easy to orchestrate, harvest your sprouting seeds a few at a time so you can eat them at different stages of their development. Start by eating them as sprouts then end when they have grown leafy shoots.

Soaking the seeds

To start the sprouting process, place the seeds in water. This is the 'soaking' stage, which 'revives' the seed and eliminates enzyme inhibitors; enzymes provide natural protection during storage and prevent out-of-season sprouting. This is why rinsing is essential to eliminate these components.

Be careful about the quality of the water. It is best to use pure water, spring water, filtered or even osmosed water.

The soaking time is sometimes quite short: 2 to 3 hours is all you need to start the germination of whole sesame or sunflower, for example. These seeds are eaten as soon as the little sprout appears.

Page 20 gives you an idea of how long soaking takes.

Soaking is not needed for:
• Basil
• Cress
• Flax
• Mustard
• Purslane
• Rocket

Soak for half a day:
• Alfalfa
• Broccoli
• Celery
• Cabbage
• Spinach
• Red lentils
• Turnip
• Radish (red, white or black)
• Buckwheat
• Whole sesame
• Hulled sunflower
• Quinoa

Soak over night:
• Dill
• Garlic
• Oats
• Wheat (spelt, kamut)
• Carrot
• Chervil
• Coriander
• Pumpkin
• Fennel
• Fenugreek
• Green lentils
• Onion
• Parsley
• Leek

For some seeds, soaking takes a bit longer. A night and half a day is needed for:
• Adzuki
• Chick peas
• Rice
• Green soya (mung beans)
These sprouts are mostly for cooking (gently and very briefly), apart from green soya (mung beans).

Soaking seeds in water starts off the germination process. Seeds where the sprout has appeared or is about to appear are easier to digest and therefore cook more quickly. For these reasons, pulses like adzuki, green lentils or chick peas are better soaked before cooking.

On the same basis, you can also pre-germinate grains for cooking, like amaranth, millet, buckwheat or quinoa. Soak them at least over night before cooking them either in a steamer or in a heavy-bottom cocotte over a low heat.

On the practical level, the seeds you put to soak can be consumed in different ways. If you soak a bowl of chick peas, some of them can be cooked and thus simply pre-germinated, whereas the rest can continue their development and be eaten as sprouted seeds.

You can thus optimise the soaking stages by having pulses (or grains) for cooking and pulses (or grains) for eating sprouted.

THE EXAMPLE OF CHICK PEAS

Put a bowl of chick peas to soak for a night and half a day, and next day, rinse and change the water. Take off three quarters of the seeds and put them to cook (for making hummus, vegetable curry, couscous, etc).

Cook gently (in a heavy-bottomed dish) for at least 45 minutes. These seeds will be simply pre-germinated.

For the remaining chick peas, start a proper germination. Rinse them regularly. After 3 days, they will be ready to eat. This time, you can steam some of them gently to make a salad or put them with rice, and the cooking will take less than a quarter of an hour.

For the sprouted chick peas that you want to eat raw, simply blanch them in boiling water.

Cooking chick peas gently (after soaking for 1 night and half a day)

Pre-sprouting and adding the emollient power of seaweed and herbs to the digestive properties will transform your cooking habits!

1 bowl of chick peas – 20 to 30 g fresh kombu seaweed preserved in salt – 1 bay leaf, a pinch of savory or a pinch of cumin or caraway

- Put a small bowl of chick peas into a salad bowl and cover with plenty of water (at least two small bowls).
- Leave to soak over night. The chick peas will swell up. Next day, rinse, change the water and leave to soak for another few hours.
- Before cooking, rinse again; the seed will be starting to show a sprout.
- Tip them into a heavy-bottomed casserole dish, cover with water and place over a low heat.
- Rinse a piece of fresh kombu preserved in salt. Cut it into little pieces using kitchen scissors or on a chopping board with a sharp knife.
- Add the seaweed to the chick peas to make them more tender. A bay leaf and a branch of savory are all the seasoning you need. To give the dish a more Oriental flavour, use a few cumin or caraway seeds.
- Continue to cook over a low heat for about 45 minutes.

Steaming chick peas (after 3 days' germination)

- Put a small bowl of chick peas into a salad bowl, cover with plenty of water (at least two small bowlsful).
- Soak over night; the chick peas will swell up. Next day, rinse, change the water and leave to soak for a further few hours.
- Rinse and drain. Spread the chick peas out on a radish plate (a plate with little holes in it) or a large (non-metallic), flat-bottomed sieve. You should spread them out in a single layer without piling them up. Three or four times a day, pass the plate under cold water to rinse and water the chick peas. Empty the excess of water that gathers in the plate underneath: don't let the water stagnate there. The chick pea sprouts will become more prominent and grow to about 0.5 cm, at which point they are ready to eat.
- Rinse and tip the sprouted chick peas into the steamer basket and steam gently in a heavy-bottomed cocotte. Ten minutes is enough; they will be soft and tender.

Chick peas to eat raw

- After 3 days' germination, sprouted chick peas can be eaten almost raw.
- Heat a casserole of water. When it boils, tip the sprouted chick peas into it to blanch them just for a few seconds. Drain.
- They are ready to eat.

Choosing a germinator

To start growing sprouts, you will find different sorts of germinators in health food shops to help you organise your own production of sprouted seeds.

3-TIER GERMINATOR

This type of germinator consists of plastic trays with drainage holes arranged in 3 layers for staggered production.

Plexiglas models seem to be more compatible with food use, because they are easy to wash and you can rinse the seeds easily.

Make sure you choose a model where the germination layers also allow for good air circulation.

After every crop, you should clean the germinator carefully with a brush right into the corners (from this point of view, round trays are more practical) and perforations.

MINI-GREENHOUSE GERMINATORS

This type of tiered Plexiglas germinator is not just aesthetically pleasing, it also allows you to grow in bulk and watch the seedlings' progress. For family use. The size and shape of the perforations in the trays vary depending on the brand and prevent the seeds getting stuck.

EARTHENWARE GERMINATORS

These have the advantage of being made in a healthy material. Earthenware regulates humidity naturally and 'breathes'. But as for all germinators, don't forget to water and spray the seeds at regular intervals to stop the roots that worm their way into the holes from drying out.

Make sure there is plenty of air circulating and brush out all the barrels carefully after every crop.

CERAMIC BARRELS WITH LITTLE POINTS

In these germinators, the plates are studded with little points that hold the sprouts when the seedlings begin to grow. Suitable for all seedlings (alfalfa type) and small-scale production (for one person).

STANDS FOR JARS WITH PIERCED LIDS

This is the most basic way of growing seeds in the kitchen. It is a simple, space-saving method and you can put the jars next to the sink to remind you to rinse them and keep them moist. It works very well for the seeds that sprout most easily: alfalfa, red and green lentils, mung beans, etc. Avoid shaking the jars too much once the shoots have appeared to avoid damaging them.

Depending on the brand, the perforated lids are made of stainless steel or plastic. You should at all costs avoid lids with grills made of oxidising metal.

"GERMINATOR TREE"

This is a special type of germinator designed for mucilaginous seeds. It consists of an earthenware stand covered with a fine layer of cotton fabric which the growing seedlings stick to and form a sticky gel. This is the case for flax, purslane, cress and basil seeds, which are thus kept moist by capillary action. Quite a specific germinator for experienced amateurs.

GERMINATORS WITH FITTED AUTOMATIC WATERING

An innovative design that does everything for you. Timer, pump, carbon filter and watering duct are all fitted in an earthenware or stainless steel cocotte and the seeds are watered automatically with filtered water.

The little shoots look vigorous and appetising and glisten with 'dew'. The financial investment is of an entirely different order compared with other germinators. You will only want to make the investment if you are totally committed to living nutrition. The yield of fresh sprouts will be such that they are likely to feature at every meal.

The machine automatically maintains a constant temperature and carefully tends the sprouts and shoots by spraying them with water.

HOME-MADE GERMINATORS

You can just as easily start the big sprouting adventure using nothing other than a glass jar and a sieve.

An improvement on this method is to cover a glass jar with a piece of muslin secured by an elastic band or with a plastic lid perforated with holes.

'Radish plates' (pierced with little holes) also allow you to experiment with sprouts. You can buy them from craft ceramicists or as part of certain dinner services.

Note that germinators with germinating trays or barrels are in fact better for the growing shoots, whereas germination in jars involves shaking the sprouting seeds every time you rinse them.

How to sprout alfalfa

This is my favourite as an introduction to sprouting. It takes about 4 days to germinate, you get quick results and it tastes nice.

For a harvest of a good handful of alfalfa shoots, put 2 heaped tablespoonfuls of seeds in a jam jar, cover with plenty of spring water and leave to soak for half a day.

Next, place a piece of muslin over the mouth of the jar to act as a filter, secure with an elastic band, and rinse and drain.

Several times a day, rinse the seeds by pouring spring water through the muslin then emptying it out to leave a moist atmosphere. Turn the jar and lay it flat so that the moist seeds stick to the sides.

To start with (the first day), you can put the jar in a place with not much light, then transfer it to a light spot (natural light) but away from direct sunlight to allow the shoots to go green. Choose a spot where you can look after the seeds easily. Whenever you think of it (2 to 5 times a day), pour a little water into the jar, rinse and drain.

If the sprouting seeds look cramped in the jar, spread them out on a radish plate (a plate with little holes in it) or a wide, non-metallic sieve and cover with a glass lid making sure that enough air is circulating around the edge to keep the atmosphere moist.

The shoots are about 2 centimetres when little green leaves start to appear. Delicate and translucent, these little shoots can be eaten when they reach a height of 2 to 3 cm.

How to sprout hulled sunflower seeds

The advantage of sunflower seeds is that they can be eaten as soon as the shoot appears. The process is very quick and they can be eaten either as sprouts or as shoots, giving you two very different treats to enjoy.

Hulled sunflower seeds take about 3 days to germinate.

Put 4 heaped tablespoonfuls of sunflower seeds in a jam jar and cover with plenty of bottled spring water. Leave to soak for half a day.

When they have soaked for a few hours, rinse them rubbing the seeds between your fingers as you do. Little husks will come away and float to the surface making them easy to get rid of during rinsing. You can eat them at this stage, just soaked.

Drain, place a piece of muslin over the mouth of the jar and secure with an elastic band to create a moist environment.

Tip the jar so that the moist seeds stick along the sides. Turn it upside down and leave it in a tilted position to prevent any water stagnating. You can prop it against the wall with the mouth resting on the lid, for instance.

You can also spread the drained seeds on a plate with a glass lid over them.

Over the next few days, continue to rinse and water with bottled spring water twice a day.

You can start to eat the seeds when the sprouts have formed and are less than half a centimetre. If you wait another day or two and use unhulled sunflower seeds, two little green leaves will appear; you can eat these shoots, too.

How to sprout lentils

Put 5 to 6 tablespoonfuls of green lentils (Puy lentils have a more concentrated and distinctive flavour) into a bowl and rinse carefully to remove any little grains of sand or grit.

Put the lentils in a jam jar, cover with bottled spring water (at least three times their volume, as they will swell up) and leave to soak over night.

Next day, rinse them until the water has lost its colour or frothiness. Leave them in the jar after tipping it so that the moist seeds stick to the glass sides. You can also spread the lentils on a plate leaving just a little moisture and cover with a glass lid. Sprinkle with spring water and rinse at least twice a day. As soon as a tiny sprout appears, you can begin to eat them.

If you find the flavour of sprouted green lentils a bit strong, a few minutes in the steamer will take the edge off it. If lentils are left to grow too long, they become fibrous and are not so nice.

If you choose red lentils, half a day's soak is sufficient.

As soon as a tiny sprout appears, you can start to eat them. Their colour is mouth-watering and the sprout makes them taste fresh and tender. They are much milder and easier to digest than green lentils. Red lentils can be eaten raw as soon as the sprout appears or when the shoot has developed and reached 2 or 3 cm.

How to sprout quinoa

Rinse the quinoa stirring the seeds, as they tend to float to the top. To begin very simply, use a large jam jar. Three or four tablespoonfuls of seeds in a jar is usually ample.

Put them in the glass jar and cover completely with bottled spring water. Place a piece of very fine cotton muslin (tulle or gauze, for example) over the jar and secure with an elastic band. As these seeds are tiny, this will make rinsing and draining easier.

Leave to soak like this for 2 to 4 hours, then rinse in spring water through the muslin or drain through a sieve. Leave them in their jar in a barely moist environment. Tip the jar so that the quinoa seeds stick to the sides. Place the jar at an angle, with the mouth pointing downwards to prevent water stagnating and allow the air to circulate.

Rinse the seeds at least twice a day. To rinse without damaging them, cover them with plenty of water so that they 'swim'. This allows the seeds to separate when they become tangled and prevents the possibility of fermentation. Drain them by spreading them along the sides of the jar to avoid them piling up. Quinoa takes between 2 to 3 days to germinate, but between the appearance of the little sprout and the growth of the first tiny leaves on the shoot, it can take 2 to 6 days. You can eat quinoa as soon as the sprout appears. Afterwards, the shoot should be eaten quickly: as soon as they reach 2 or 3 cm they tend to wither.

How to sprout fenugreek

Rinse the fenugreek seeds before soaking them in bottled spring water over night in a jar. Use about 3 or 4 tablespoonfuls of seeds.

Next day, change the water, which will have discoloured. Rinse and drain.

Place a piece of very fine cotton muslin (tulle or gauze, for example) over the jar and secure with an elastic band (or close with a lid with holes in it). Tip the jar so that the seeds stick to the sides and place the jar at an angle with the mouth pointing downwards to stop water stagnating and let the air circulate.

Rinse the seeds two or three times a day to get rid of the gel they produce and which will make them stick together.

It takes about 3 days for fenugreek to germinate. If you want to wait for the leafy shoots, continue growing and allow at least a week. When they reach this stage and if the shoot is strong, you can keep them in the fridge for a few days, as long as you 'spin-dry' the shoots. I use a little salad spinner to dry them before putting them back in a jar in the fridge.

The different sprouts

A growing seedling explodes and reaches full development in the conditions indicated in a short time. In a jar or germinator, the sprouts all reach a limit at a certain point, after which they have exhausted their reserves (because they are not in the ground). Every seed is therefore considered as having a maximum size at which to be eaten for the optimal level of nutrients.

This is something you feel and depends on the conditions in which the seeds are put to germinate. You will learn to recognise the best moments to eat them or to stop the sprouting process.

Germination times vary according to the temperature of the room, time of year, the way you water them, and so on. Consequently, I don't always indicate times. A pumpkin, for instance, takes a day, whereas fennel or coriander takes ten days. I tend to prefer to give the size of the sprouted seed at maturity to give an idea of the best moment for picking.

ADZUKI This pulse can be soaked for pre-germination (which makes them easier to digest) and can then be given a gentle cook. Sprouted seeds that have reached 0.5 cm can be eaten raw.

ALFALFA Alfalfa seeds are easy to grow and eaten when they are about 3 cm. They are pretty and delicate with a mild flavour that everyone likes. You should rinse the shoots well to get rid of their brown husk.

BROCCOLI The shoots can be eaten when they reach 2 to 3 cm. To develop the chlorophyll, place them in daylight after the 3rd or 4th day.

BUCKWHEAT A pretty, multifaceted seed. The whole, hulled seeds (kasha, which is toasted, i.e. pre-cooked, buckwheat is not suitable) are soaked and rinsed thoroughly, as the water will become viscous. For successful germination, buckwheat should be well drained, as it requires little water. You need only wait 2 or 3 days before eating, when the sprout will have reached a few millimetres.

RED CABBAGE The little shoots are a pretty colour and can be eaten when they are 2 to 3 cm. To make their distinctive flavour milder, they are best mixed with other shoots, like alfalfa.

CARROTS These are not the easiest seeds to sprout and germination takes more than a week. Carrots can be eaten when the shoots are at least 4 cm long and the leaves are showing.

CELERY These fragrant shoots can be eaten when they are 2 cm.

CHICK PEAS These are soaked for pre-germination to soften them then cooked gently in the ordinary way.

Chick peas are only eaten as sprouts of about 0.5 cm and they should be cooked briefly: the sprouted seeds should be just blanched or steamed for a few minutes to make them easier to digest. Sprouted chick peas have a delicate flavour and melting texture. Sprouting limit: maximum of 3 days.

CRESS These seeds are mucilaginous and form a gel when they come into contact with water. They are less suited to being grown in a jar and you should choose a tray, place them on cotton fabric or use a 'germinator tree'. They can be eaten when the shoots are about 4 cm after exposing them to daylight to develop the chlorophyll.

DILL The shoots can be eaten at about 2 or 3 cm. They have a fresh, aniseed flavour. A real aromatic delight.

FENNEL Mild and scented, fennel shoots can be eaten when they reach 3 cm. Their aniseed flavour makes a very pleasant addition.

FENUGREEK When the seeds are put to soak, they produce quite a powerful spicy smell. It dissipates during germination. The soaked seeds also produce a kind of gel. Fenugreek sprouted seeds can be eaten after about 3 days' germination and have a strongish flavour. If you want to wait for the little leaves, you should leave seeds to germinate for at least a week, at which point the shoot will be about 2 cm. They have a very pleasant aromatic smell.

FLAX The seeds produce a sticky gel on contact with water. These mucilaginous seeds are ideal for growing on a germinator tree. You can eat them when just sprouted or as 4-cm high shoots.

GARLIC You can eat the shoots at about 3 or 4 cm. They have a distinctive flavour and should be added sparingly to dishes. Garlic shoots are thought to be easier to digest than cloves.

LEEKS A tiny black seed that takes time to wake up, so allow about ten days. The shoots can be eaten from 3 to 4 cm. They have a distinctive flavour that will spice up a dish and a little pinch is enough.

GREEN LENTILS Soak them for pre-germination to make them easier to digest, then cook them gently. They are easy to grow as both sprouted seed a few millimetres' long and as leafy shoots. The raw sprouts have quite a strong flavour. To take the edge off it and make them easier to digest, you can steam them gently for 5 minutes. The shoots can be eaten when they are 2 to 3 cm. Make sure you rinse them thoroughly to remove the husks protecting the seeds.

RED LENTILS These germinate easily and are very nice to eat raw as soon as the sprouts appear (2 or 3 mm). They should be rinsed thoroughly until the cloudy water turns clear. They are easier to digest than the green variety, so you don't have to blanch the sprouts first. They also have a higher iron and calcium content. Like green lentils, they can be eaten as sprouts or shoots.

WHOLE MILLET The round, unhulled seeds will produce green shoots that can be eaten at around 2 or 3 cm.

MUNG BEANS These are commonly called 'soya sprouts' or 'soya shoots' because they belong to the green soya family. Green soya is very different from yellow soya, which is more widely known and used to make tofu and soya milk. They have different nutritional characteristics and go through different transformations. To avoid confusion, what used to be called 'soya sprouts' are now frequently called 'mung bean shoots'. They are easy to germinate and are eaten when the shoots reach 2 or 3 cm (cf. green soya).

MUSTARD Eat the shoots when they are about 4 cm to enjoy their characteristic piquancy.

OATS Sprouted oats can be eaten as soon as they germinate or you can wait for the young shoots to form. Eat the sprouts raw or steam them briefly. Wait till the shoots reach 2 cm before eating.

ONION The small black seeds of onions produce bright green shoots about 2 cm high that have a piquant flavour.

BLACK RADISH The shoots are about 2 or 3 cm when picked. They have a strong, distinctive flavour and should be added sparingly to salads. Ideally, radish seeds should accompany other sprouted seeds with milder shoots (such as alfalfa).

PINK RADISH The green shoots have a sharp, peppery flavour. Use them as you would a herb to spice a dish or mix them with other sprouted seeds. Eat them at about 3 cm.

BROWN RICE Eat the sprouted seeds as soon as they germinate or as shoots about 2 cm high. In both cases, it is best to cook them briefly, either steamed or sautéed in a wok along with other vegetables.

ROCKET When the shoots are about 3 cm they are characterised by a very pronounced flavour. The mucilaginous seeds are not suitable for sprouting in a jar, and it is best to choose a tray or germinator tree. Add sparingly to salads. Ideal with mesclun. When cooked very briefly in hot broth, their flavour becomes milder.

WHOLE SESAME Soak the day before, then eat 'pre-germinated' or when the sprout is barely 1 mm. Germination limit: maximum 2 days, after which they tend to become bitter.

GREEN SOYA Sprouts that are commonly called 'soya' come from mung beans, a variety of green soya (as distinct from yellow soya which is used for making soya milk and tofu). Soya sprouts are eaten when well grown. Remove the green skins first for a milder taste (cf. mung bean).

SUNFLOWER Hulled sunflower seeds are easy to germinate and eat. They are mild and tender as sprouts a few millimetres' long. When you rinse the seeds, rub them gently to remove most of the skins. With unhulled seeds, if the sunflower seeds reach the stage of shoots, two little bright green leaves will appear at about 3 cm.

SPROUT BREAD: ESSENE BREAD

Essene bread is made with sprouted grain that has been reduced to a purée and the resulting dough dried at a low heat for several hours.

This is a dense, energy-rich bread that keeps well for several weeks, while essene bread rolls are ideal for taking on excursions. You will find them ready-made in health food shops. Sometimes raisins or other dried fruit or oil seeds have been mixed with the sprout dough to make the bread sweeter. On the same basis, you can make grain biscuits to replace the bread. The grains are germinated then blended and the resulting dough is rolled out thinly and dried in the oven at a very low temperature for several hours. If you want to try your hand at this recipe, see the books on the subject (cf. Bibliography).

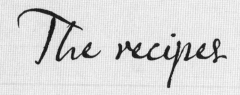

The recipes

Unless otherwise indicated, the proportions are for 4 people.

MEASUREMENTS

You should choose a 15 cl glass.

COOKING

Cooking time in the oven and the temperature indication are for an electric oven. The thermostat / degrees Celsius relation is 30 ° (i.e., Mark 6 = 180°). Unless otherwise indicated, the recipes do not require the oven to be preheated.

Cooking time for steamed recipes or recipes in a saucepan with the lid on are given for cooking in heavy-bottomed cocottes or frying pans suitable for gentle cooking, in order to preserve the vitamins and minerals.

All the ingredients used in the recipes are readily available in shops or health food cooperatives.

For some recipes that use margarine, preference is given to non-hydrogenated dairy-free margarine.

NB: In my recipes, I have chosen to avoid milk products and provided non-dairy alternatives. But if you prefer to use cow's milk, the proportions will be the same: follow the instructions given for dairy-free milk.

Sprouts as Appetizers

Tomato juice with fennel

Peel and deseed the tomatoes. Chop them up and put them in the liquidizer goblet with the sprouted fennel seed shoots. Use one to two tablespoons fennel shoots per tomato. Blend to a fine purée, dilute with water and add a pinch of salt. Serve immediately.

You can also make tomato juice by putting them whole into the juicer. Enjoy immediately with a few shoots of sprouted fennel seed sprinkled on top: use one tablespoon per glass of tomato juice.

Juice of spring carrots with alfalfa

Wash the carrots and place them in the juicer. Decorate each glass of carrot juice with a pinch of alfalfa shoots.

Carrot and celery juice with fenugreek

Wash half a dozen carrots and chop a stick of celery into chunks. Put the vegetables in the juicer. Sprinkle a pinch of sprouted fenugreek shoots on each glass of juice to make it a treat for the eye as well as the palate.

Red cocktail

Wash 4 carrots and peel 1 small raw beetroot (the size of an orange). Put the vegetables in the juicer. Place a tablespoonful of sprouted red cabbage shoots to give a pretty colour.

Crudités and sprouted wheat on toast

For a thoroughly springtime aperitif, replace the toast with discs of carrot and use different sprouted seeds to garnish.

2 carrots
A dozen radishes
3 tablespoons cashew nut purée
6 heaped tablespoons sprouted wheat

Peel the carrots. Clean the radishes.

Slice the vegetables into discs. Cut the radishes diagonally to make the slices bigger.

Put the cashew nut purée into a small bowl, salt lightly and dilute with just a tablespoon of water, then stir in the sprouted wheat. Mix everything together thoroughly and place a knob on each vegetable slice.

You can also put this mixture in the blender to obtain a homogenous pâté that should be eaten immediately.

Seaweed and alfalfa on puffed rice toast

These puffed rice biscuits have a delicate flavour that make them ideal as a base for spreads and garnishes. They are also available in combinations of rice and buckwheat, rice and quinoa or rice and lentils, giving them a slightly more pronounced flavour.

5 or 6 puffed rice biscuits
Dairy-free margarine or blanched almond purée
Fleur de sel or pink salt
1 piece of fresh seaweed preserved in salt
5 tablespoons sprouted alfalfa shoots

Rinse and dry the seaweed (a teaspoonful). Crumple a piece in your hand and using kitchen scissors or a sharp knife on a chopping board, cut it into small pieces.

Spread the puffed rice biscuits with a thin layer of dairy-free margarine or blanched almond purée, then garnish with chopped seaweed.

Spread with the flat of a knife. Sprinkle a few grains of *fleur de sel* or pink salt over it followed by a few pinches of alfalfa shoots.

Polenta with sesame

In this recipe for appetizer canapés, the pre-germinated sesame turns soft and adds a mild note.

125 g polenta (ground maize)
1/2 litre water
1 teaspoon salt
90 g whole sesame

Half a day ahead, soak the sesame in bottled spring water. Rinse using a fine sieve.

Make the polenta: put the ground maize into a saucepan, thin with cold water and place over a low heat. Stir frequently until the polenta thickens. Leave to cook gently for 10 minutes.

Salt the polenta, take it off the heat and add the pre-germinated sesame. Spread a layer of polenta 1 cm thick over an oiled glass or porcelain baking tray. Leave to cool, and place in the fridge.

A few hours later when the polenta is firm, cut it into cubes and arrange them upside down (smooth side up, i.e., the one that was resting on the oiled baking tray) on plates with cocktail sticks in them. They can also be served as a main course with lettuce.

Mousse with hazelnuts and fenugreek

A nutty paste for spreading on toast or garnishing endive leaves as an appetizer. Add a pinch of sprouts to decorate and make them tastier. Variant: the fenugreek can be replaced by alfalfa.

235 g pot thick soya cream
4 tablespoons hazelnut oil
1/2 glass whole shelled hazelnuts
6 heaped tablespoons sprouted fenugreek shoots
2 or 3 chicory heads or slices of toast (spelt bread)

Dry fry the whole, shelled hazelnuts to brown them. When they are cool, chop them roughly in a blender to obtain finely crushed hazelnuts.

Add the hazelnut oil to the thick soya cream, salt lightly and add the chopped hazelnuts.

Cut the base from the chicory and carefully remove the leaves. Garnish each leaf with a small spoonful of the mousse. Or spread on slices of wholemeal toast.

Sprinkle a good pinch of fenugreek shoots on each slice/ leaf.

Vegetable dip

A creamy saucc for crudités to serve cold at a buffet.

3 tablespoons cashew nut purée
400 g pot soya fromage blanc
5 tablespoons sprouted sesame
Salt

Assortment of crudités:
1 or 2 carrots
1 courgette
1 celery stick

Pour the cashew nut purée into a bowl. It should be sufficiently liquid (room temperature) to mix it easily. Add three or four spoonfuls of dairy-free fromage blanc and stir well to obtain a thick cream. Season with salt and add the rest of the soya fromage blanc. Stir. Put in the fridge until just before serving.

At the last minute, stir in the sprouted sesame seeds.

Wash the vegetables, cut them into matchsticks and arrange them in a dish. Offer the dip as an accompaniment.

Cream of avocado with sprouted sunflower seeds

A guacamole-type cream, enhanced by tender sunflower seeds. Variant: they can be added after blending the avocado if you prefer the crisp contrast of the whole seeds.

2 avocados
Juice of half a lemon
Herb salt
4 heaped tablespoons sprouted sunflower seeds
1 small white onion

Cut the avocados into quarters, remove their skin and stone, then put the pieces into a blender. Add the lemon juice, salt, peeled onion and the sprouted sunflower seeds.

Reduce to a purée and serve immediately to spread on toast or present as a dip for crudités.

Paprika and red cabbage canapés

Arranged on a tray as an appetizer, these polenta canapés are browned in olive oil and topped with a knob of paprika cream and a pinch of red cabbage shoots.

125 g polenta (ground maize)
¹/₂ litre water
1 teaspoon salt
Olive oil

6 to 8 tablespoons sprouted red cabbage seed shoots
6 tablespoons thick soya cream
2 pinches paprika
Salt

Put the ground maize into a casserole dish, add the cold water and place over a low heat. Stir frequently until the polenta thickens. Leave to cook gently for 10 minutes. Season with salt and pour into a greased round mould. Place in the fridge.

When the polenta has cooled, it becomes firm and can be cut into slices.

Pour a little olive oil into a large frying pan and brown the polenta discs. Repeat several times allowing 2 or 3 spoonfuls of oil per pan. Lay the slices of polenta on a paper towel. Leave to cool.

Make the sauce by stirring the salt and paprika vigorously into the soya cream.

Drop a knob of cream on each slice of polenta and finish with a pinch of red cabbage shoots. Serve immediately.

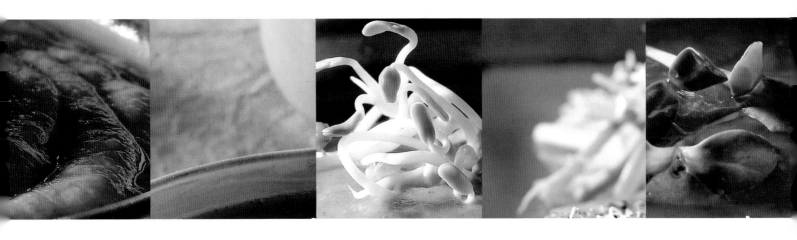

Sprouts in vegetable soups and veloutés

Pea and radish velouté

Peas make a delicious velouté, and their sweetish flavour is complemented by the piquancy of the radish shoots while the oil adds a milder, rounder note.

800 g fresh peas
5 tablespoons shoots sprouted radish
4 tablespoons sesame oil
Salt

Heat a casserole dish of water. When it boils, tip in the peas. Leave to cook for 5 to 10 minutes.

Put the peas in the liquidizer and just cover with part of the cooking water. Season with salt and blend to obtain a rich, creamy velouté.

Pour into soup bowls, drizzle with a little sesame oil and arrange a dome of sprouted radish seed shoots.

Velouté of aniseed carrots

The flavour of the carrots harmonises with the aniseed of the fennel shoots.

5 carrots
The white part of 1 leek
5 heaped tablespoons sprouted fennel seed shoots
4 tablespoons safflower oil

Brush the carrots and slice into discs; do the same with the leek. Cover with boiling water and cook over a low heat for less than 20 minutes.

Blend to a fine velouté, salt lightly and pour into soup bowls.

Place a dome of sprouted fennel seed shoots in the centre of the bowls and finish with a drizzle of oil.

Chinese broth with mung bean sprouts

Mung bean shoots are commonly known as 'soya sprouts'. You can vary this recipe by adding a handful of rice vermicelli to make a thicker broth.

1.5 litres water
1 onion
1 carrot
2 fresh shiitake mushrooms
2 tablespoons dried seaweed flakes
5 tablespoons mung bean sprouts
50 g tofu
Salt
Soy sauce
Optional: a few fresh coriander leaves

Bring the water to the boil. Grate the onion and carrot. Slice the mushrooms thinly. Tip the vegetables and seaweed flakes into the boiling water. Cook for 10 minutes.

Cut the tofu into tiny cubes with half-centimetre sides and add them to the broth with the soy sprouts. Off the heat, salt the soup very lightly as everyone will add the soy sauce according to their taste. Scatter with chopped coriander.

Serve hot.

Velouté of courgettes and fenugreek

This velouté of courgettes is served as a mild cream with a hint of turmeric. As an accompaniment, I suggest sprouted fenugreek shoots for their powerful flavour and Oriental aroma.

1 kg courgettes
2 glasses water (300 ml)
4 tablespoons sprouted fenugreek shoots
1 tablespoon olive oil
Salt
Pinch turmeric

Wash the courgettes and cut into discs. Put the olive oil and turmeric into a heavy-bottomed casserole, stir over a low heat for a few seconds, then add the courgettes and water. Cover and cook for 20 minutes.

When the courgettes are tender, put them with the cooking juices into the liquidizer. Add salt and reduce to a cream. If the mixture is too thick, add a little water.

Serve hot and sprinkle sprouted fenugreek shoots on each portion.

Tomato soup with red lentil sprouts

Red lentil sprouts are crisp with a mild flavour. They enhance this tomato soup, which the cream of quinoa makes thick and fragrant.

6 very ripe tomatoes
4 tablespoons olive oil
1 bay leaf
1 pinch marjoram
3 tablespoons cream of quinoa (precooked flour)
300 ml water
Salt
4 heaped tablespoons sprouted red lentils

Peel the tomatoes. If they are very ripe, the skin will come away easily, otherwise put them in the steamer basket for a few minutes.

Chop them up and heat them in a casserole dish with olive oil and the bay leaf and pinch of marjoram for ten minutes, stirring frequently.

Dilute the cream of quinoa in a bowl by adding the water a little at a time. Pour in the tomatoes and stir until the cream of quinoa creates a homogenous soup. Season with salt, remove the bay leaf, pour into the liquidizer and reduce to a velouté.

Serve hot in bowls and sprinkle with sprouted red lentils.

Gazpacho of red peppers and two sunflowers

A creamy velouté that can be served as an aperitif in little glasses or as a first course with pieces of toast. The sunflower seeds are used here as sprouts blended into the soup and as shoots for decoration. A way of enjoying the sprouts at two different stages of their development.

3 red peppers
3 tablespoons olive oil
1 garlic clove
1 glass 150 ml water
Salt
6 tablespoons sprouted sunflower seeds
4 tablespoons sunflower seed shoots
Optional: argan oil

Cut the red peppers into strips and place them in a heavy-bottomed cocotte over a low heat with the garlic clove and olive oil. After ten minutes, stir to coat the peppers thoroughly, and add the glass of water.

Continue to cook over a low heat. When the peppers are tender, pour them with the cooking juices and sprouted sunflower seeds into a liquidizer. Add salt and reduce to a cream.

Serve warm or cold in goblets and decorate with sunflower seed shoots. Drizzle a little argan oil over the gazpacho. The warm fragrance of the oil will evoke the smells of southern cooking.

Cream of leeks with garlic

This leek velouté gets its creamy consistency from the silky tofu, which is like firm custard and can be bought ready packaged at the chilled health food aisle. The garlic shoots enhance the flavours and I add slivered almonds for a crispy contrast.

3 leeks
Salt
1/2 teaspoon turmeric
2 tablespoons olive oil
400 g silky tofu
3 tablespoons shoots of sprouted garlic
3 tablespoons slivered almonds

Cut and wash the leeks and slice them into discs. Pour the olive oil and turmeric into a heavy-bottomed cocotte, place over a low heat and stir to heat the spice. Add the leeks, cover and leave to cook with the lid on over a low heat for 15 to 20 minutes.

Put the silky tofu into the liquidizer, season with salt and add the cooked leeks. Blend to a cream and pour into the casserole dish to reheat the mixture gently without boiling.

Put the slivered almond into a dry frying pan over a low heat; they will brown in a few seconds.

Pour the cream of leeks into little bowls or glasses and sprinkle with a few shoots of sprouted garlic seeds and slivered almond.

Sprouted lentils minestrone

Soups of diced vegetables easily accommodate legume sprouts. The result is a highly nutritious soup.

2 courgettes
1 carrot
2 handfuls French beans
1 handful pasta (macaroni, shell shapes, etc)
3 tablespoons olive oil
A few basil leaves
5 heaped tablespoons sprouted green lentils

Boil two litres of water, then plunge in the French beans with the strings removed and cut into chunks one or two centimetres' long. Next, add the courgettes unpeeled and diced, as well as the carrot, also diced.

Continue to cook them over a low heat for 10 minutes then add a handful of pasta and season with salt. Remove from the heat when they are *al dente*.

Chop the basil leaves into the hot soup, add the sprouted lentils and pour in a drizzle of olive oil. Serve hot immediately.

Sprout Sauces and Dressings

Tamari salad dressing with sprouted sunflower seeds

An alternative to vinaigrette, this is a dressing with a pleasant texture that resembles a thick mustard dressing.

Its piquant flavour makes it an ideal accompaniment to chicory leaves, steamed leeks, frisée lettuce, grated carrots and beetroots, etc.

5 tablespoons sunflower seed sprouts
1 tablespoon tamari (soy sauce)
2 tablespoons sunflower oil
Juice of half a lemon

In a herb mill, crush the sprouted sunflower seeds and add the tamari. Then stir in the sunflower oil and lemon juice as required.

Blend well to obtain a thick, creamy consistency.

Sprouted red lentil dressing

Walnut oil and fragrant cumin go well with tender, melting red lentil sprouts. A dressing to pour over grains (rice, buckwheat, quinoa, etc) or to use with crudités (grated beetroots or carrots, or lettuce).

6 tablespoons red lentil sprouts
4 tablespoons walnut oil
Salt
2 pinches ground cumin

Rinse and drain the sprouted lentils.

Mix the walnut oil, cumin and salt in a small bowl and add the red lentils. Mix well and serve with a grain.

Sesame sprout mayonnaise

Entirely dairy-free, this dressing is made like a mayonnaise and is the perfect accompaniment to steamed vegetables, especially pumpkins, squashes or courgettes, carrots and broccoli or jacket potatoes.

3 heaped tablespoons blanched almond purée
Juice of half a lemon
3 to 8 tablespoons rice milk
1 tablespoon sprouted sesame
Salt

Pour the blanched almond purée and lemon juice into the liquidizer goblet and blend briefly. The almond purée will become very thick, so add three tablespoons rice milk to make the dressing. Season with salt and add a little more rice milk. Blend briefly again.

Add a little rice milk if the dressing is too thick, never blend for long.

This mayonnaise can be made in a few seconds. When it reaches the consistency you want, add the well-drained sesame sprouts. Stir together.

Coral-coloured winter coulis

This pumpkin coulis is delicious when the pumpkin has a dense flesh that produces a tender pulp. I use this dressing to pour over dairy-free burgers, pasta and all sorts of grains.

800 g pumpkin or squash
White part of 1 leek
250 g button mushrooms
2 tablespoons olive oil (optional)
Knob of dairy-free butter
3 tablespoons red lentil sprouts

Peel the pumpkin and cut little pieces into a heavy-bottomed frying pan. Add the leek sliced into discs and place over a very gentle heat with just the olive oil (optional) and three tablespoonfuls of water.

Meanwhile, cook the mushrooms. Heat the margarine in a frying pan. When it is hot, tip in the finely sliced mushrooms. Stir over a high heat. Season with salt and pepper.

When the pumpkin is cooked, it literally melts into a purée when stirred. Pour into a liquidizer goblet to obtain a smooth, thick purée.

Depending on how you want to use this dressing, the mushrooms can be added as slices in the pumpkin-leek mixture or blended at the same time (always brown them first to bring out their flavour).

At the last minute, mix the red lentil sprouts into the coulis.

Cream of white aubergines

White aubergines have a soft texture like mushrooms, especially if you heat them in olive oil with a little garlic and parsley. In this recipe, I add fenugreek shoots to spice them up a bit or garden cress if you want to retain a mild flavour.

2 white aubergines
2 garlic cloves
6 tablespoons olive oil
At least 5 tablespoons liquid soya cream
5 tablespoons sprouted fenugreek shoots (or garden cress)

Peel the aubergines (or leave the skin on if it is very thin) and dice them finely.

Put the olive oil in a frying pan, add the aubergine pieces and cloves of garlic, mix and cover. Cook over a low heat stirring from time to time until the aubergines are tender. Season with salt. Transfer them to the liquidizer goblet and reduce to a creamy sauce incorporating the liquid soya cream.

When cooked, the aubergines will have a fairly thick consistency, so add liquid soya cream as necessary.

The cream can be served warm on toast and sprinkled with sprouted fenugreek or garden cress shoots. If you are going to have it cold, mix in the shoots at the last moment and serve as an accompaniment to crudités or stuffed vegetables.

Fennel coulis with buckwheat sprouts

A light coulis to pour over vegetarian terrines, pasta, such as ravioli stuffed with tofu, or vegetables. Or you can serve it as a warm velouté in little glasses as an appetizer before a meal. The buckwheat sprouts are mild and their slightly floury flavour goes well with the fennel blended to a creamy sauce.

2 small fennel bulbs (about 300 g)
4 tablespoons buckwheat sprouts
Herb salt

Slice the end off the fennel stalks if they are a bit fibrous and cut off the base pulling the side strings off as you do.

Cut the bulbs into quarters and steam for about 15 minutes.

Put 150 ml of stock under the steamer basket (if you are cooking organic fennel bulbs, you can keep the cooking juices) and pour into the liquidizer goblet. Add the fennel bulbs and blend to obtain a liquid purée.

Pour into side dishes and sprinkle with buckwheat sprouts.

Hollandaise sauce with mustard seed sprouts

A light sauce in which the full-bodied, piquant flavours of mustard shoots are a pleasant surprise. This soya-based sauce (silky tofu is a malleable tofu with the consistency of custard and comes ready packaged in the chilled section of health food shops) can balance a grain dish accompanied with steamed vegetables.

200 g silky tofu
100 g olive oil
Salt and pepper
$1/2$ teaspoon turmeric
3 tablespoons mustard seed shoots

Put the liquidizer goblet on the scales to measure out the silky tofu and also pour in 50 g of the olive oil. Blend for a few seconds to obtain a smooth consistency.

Season with salt, pepper and the turmeric then add the remaining 50 g olive oil. Blend thoroughly. The mixture will swell and froth up. Check the seasoning is to your taste.

Pour into a bowl and set aside in the fridge until you want to serve it. Just before you bring it to the table, stir in the mustard seed shoots.

See page 100 in the chapter Sprouts and dairy-free 'cheese': Fromage frais with shoots.

Sprouts in raw dishes

Mesclun salad with flat leaf parsley

A light sweet and sour dressing is used to coat this salad of sprouted shoots. As a variant, making the dressing with umeboshi prune juice (see recipe on page 82) is just as good.

1 salad bowl of mesclun salad (a mix of lettuce and
    dandelion leaves)
1 small bunch flat leaf parsley
5 to 6 heaped tablespoons leafy shoots of your choice:
    alfalfa, fenugreek, fennel, red cabbage, rocket,
    garden cress, for example

For the dressing:
1 tablespoon balsamic vinegar
1 tablespoon rice syrup
4 to 5 tablespoons olive oil
Salt

Stir together the rice syrup and balsamic vinegar and thin by adding the oil a little at a time. Season with salt.

Tip the salad leaves into the bowl, strip the parsley leaves and scatter with the leafy sprouts. Stir in the dressing and serve immediately.

Salad of spinach leaves and sunflower seed sprouts with lemon dressing

You can also add a few salad leaves to this mixture or replace the lamb's lettuce with other lettuce.

1 handful rocket
1 handful tender spinach leaves (the centre leaves)
2 handful lamb's lettuce
5 tablespoons sunflower seed sprouts

For the dressing:
1 teaspoon lemon juice
4 to 5 tablespoons sunflower oil
Salt

Wash the spinach and pick out only the young leaves from the centre, which are small and tender.

In a salad bowl, prepare the dressing by emulsifying the lemon juice with the oil. Season lightly with salt. After rinsing the lamb's lettuce and rocket, dry all the leaves in the salad spinner and toss them in the dressing. Sprinkle with sunflower seed sprouts.

Sprout salad with tofu

Cubes of lacto-fermented tofu and sprouts make this an energy-rich salad with high levels of enzymes and vitamins. Lacto-fermented tofu can be found mixed with vegetables and preserved in oil (chilled health food aisle).

1 frisée lettuce
6 tablespoons sunflower seed sprouts
4 tablespoons alfalfa (or fennel) shoots
200 g pot preserved lacto-fermented tofu in marinade

Wash and prepare the salad leaves. Dice the tofu finely into a salad bowl and pour in half the marinade to act as a dressing for the salad.

Mix with the curly lettuce, alfalfa shoots and sunflower seed sprouts.

Half-and-half salad with red cabbage

The tiny rosy shoots of the red cabbage complement the bright orange, healthy colours of the grated pumpkin and carrot.

1/4 small pumpkin or squash (100 g)
2 carrots
5 or 6 full tablespoons sprouted red cabbage shoots

For the soy sauce with gomasio (sesame salt)
1 teaspoon soy sauce (tamari or shoyu)
6 teaspoons olive or sunflower oil
1 teaspoon gomasio

Add the olive oil to the soy sauce a spoonful at a time. Add the gomasio and stir well to make a smooth sauce.

Wash the young carrots.

If the skin is hard, cut the pumpkin into slices to make peeling easier. Finely grate the pumpkin and carrots. Stir in the dressing and sprinkle with red cabbage sprouts.

Spring rolls with miso peanut dressing and beetroot mousse

Each spring roll is made from rice paper with a strip of nori wrapped around it. This not only gives the rolls an original, iodised flavour, but also creates a pretty, decorative contrast in this colourful dish. The beetroot mixed with dairy-free fromage blanc turns into a fine dark red mousse, while the tiny white seeds of the sprouted quinoa nestle in the lettuce leaves.

For the beetroot mousse:
100 g raw beetroot
100 g soya fromage blanc
1 small white onion or spring onion
2 tablespoons cold pressed rape seed oil
Salt

For the salad:
1 lettuce
1 garlic clove
1 teaspoon lemon juice
3 or 4 tablespoons sunflower oil
4 heaped tablespoons quinoa sprouts

For the spring rolls:
8 sheets of fresh or rehydrated rice paper
2 sheets of nori
80 g mung bean (green soya) sprouts
200 g brown rice, cooked
200 g smoked or spicy tofu
4 heaped tablespoons sunflower seed sprouts
2 pinches paprika
Salt

For the spring rolls: In a salad bowl, mix the cooked rice with the smoked tofu which has first been crushed with a fork. Add the mung bean sprouts and sunflower seed shoots. Season with salt and paprika.

Cut each sheet of nori into four strips about 4 or 5 cm wide. If you are using dry rice paper sheets: place them on a damp cloth and moisten with water until the sheet softens before proceeding with the filling. For fresh rice sheets (which you can find in the chilled health food aisle), you don't have to bother with the re-hydration stage.

Lay a strip of nori from top to bottom down the middle of a sheet of rice paper, lining it up at the bottom. Place a few spoonfuls of stuffing on the upper part to make a horizontal dumpling. Fold the left and right sides of the sheet of rice paper over the stuffing, then fold up the bottom and roll up, packing the stuffing down with your fingers as you go to form the spring roll.

Prepare the miso peanut dressing: in a small bowl, thin the peanut purée with three tablespoons of water. Add the miso and stir well adding one or two tablespoons of water.

For the beetroot mousse: Peel the beetroot and cut it into small pieces in the chopping bowl of a food processor with the chopped spring onion. Mince the vegetables. Then add the soya fromage blanc and rape seed oil. Season with salt. Blend to obtain a homogenous cream.

For the salad: Wash the lettuce leaves. Put the sunflower oil and lemon juice in a salad bowl and add the salt and crushed garlic. Stir the dressing to coat the lettuce leaves.

To serve: lay two spring rolls on each plate and pour the miso peanut dressing over them with the lettuce sprinkled with quinoa sprouts alongside. Put a few spoonfuls of beetroot mousse in a lettuce leave.

Sprout remoulade with lacto-fermented sauerkraut

The rape seed oil softens the piquant flavour of the raw sauerkraut while the turmeric gives it a spicy fragrance. The hazelnut purée makes the sprout remoulade rich and creamy. A feast for the eyes: the beetroot and black radish are presented in fine discs around the edge of the plate.

200 g raw, lacto-fermented sauerkraut
4 tablespoons cold pressed rape seed oil
2 pinches ground turmeric
4 tablespoons sprouted fenugreek

For the sprout remoulade:
100 g mung bean (green soya) sprouts
50 g sunflower seed shoots
3 tablespoons hazelnut purée
6 tablespoons soya fromage blanc
Salt

1 red beetroot
1 small black radish

Put the rape seed oil in a salad bowl and stir in the turmeric. Add the sauerkraut and sprouted fenugreek.

In another salad bowl, prepare the remoulade. Pour in the hazelnut purée; it should be liquid enough (room temperature) to mix easily with the soya fromage blanc. Salt lightly. Mix with the mung bean sprouts and sunflower seed shoots.

Peel or wash the beetroot and black radish. Use a mandoline to slice them extremely finely. Arrange the slices all around the edge of the plate, using one half of the plate for beetroot slices and the other for the black radish.

On the radish side, arrange the sauerkraut with turmeric and sprouted fenugreek.

On the beetroot side, arrange the sprout remoulade.

Winter crudités with hazelnut milk

A drink made from hazelnuts soaked the day before, which you can serve in little glasses as an appetizer surrounded by a selection of winter vegetables. The hazelnut flavour takes several forms: fresh nuts soaked the day before for eating, the mild hazelnut milk and the creamy sauce of the concentrated purée.

4 heads chicory
1 small celeriac
300 g button mushrooms
4 to 6 heaped tablespoons sprouted red lentils
4 essene bread rolls

For the dressing for the crudités:
4 tablespoons hazelnut purée
4 tablespoons tamari (soy sauce)
8 to 10 tablespoons water

For the hazelnut milk:
200 g shelled hazelnuts

The day before, soak the nuts covering them with twice their volume of water.

Next day, prepare the hazelnut milk.

Rinse the nuts; keep back a dozen whole nuts. Put all the rest in the liquidizer goblet, cover them with water and blend to obtain a thin cream. Sieve them to collect the milk (save the pulp: you can use it to make dairy-free biscuits or to mix into a cream or cake). Pour the milk you have collected into glasses or cups.

Prepare the dressing for the crudités: thin the hazelnut purée with the soy sauce and mix with a few spoonfuls of water.

Clean the mushrooms and slice finely. Sprinkle them with lemon juice to stop them turning brown.

Peel the celeriac and grate finely. As with the mushrooms, you can stop the celeriac turning brown by mixing it with a few drops of lemon juice.

Cut the chicory into quarters lengthwise and remove the base, which can sometimes be bitter. Lay the quarters on each plate.

Arrange the crudités and red lentil sprouts on the plates and pour over the hazelnut-tamari sauce. Sprinkle with a few whole nuts roughly chopped with a knife. Add an essene bread roll. Serve the hazelnut milk on the side.

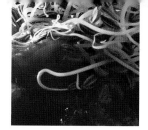

Summer tabbouleh and crudités

This dish is bursting with colour: courgette guacamole, tomatoes with sprouted fennel shoots and parsley tabbouleh with sprouted quinoa. As an accompaniment, you can choose essene cakes, which come as thin dry biscuits (pancakes) that are quite different from essene bread (which is much denser).

4 ripe tomatoes
3 tablespoons olive oil
5 tablespoons sprouted fennel shoots
2 pinches celery salt

Black olive tapenade and essene bread rolls or biscuits

For the parsley tabbouleh:
1 glass sprouted quinoa
1/2 glass sprouted sesame
1 bunch flat leaf parsley
1 white onion
4 tablespoons sesame oil

For the courgette guacamole:
3 avocados
2 tablespoons lemon juice
1 small courgette
Herb salt

Peel the tomatoes, dice the flesh finely and put the cubes into a salad bowl. Coat with olive oil and season with celery salt.

Chop the parsley and white onion finely and mix them in a salad bowl with the quinoa and sesame sprouts. Drizzle a little sesame oil over everything to coat. Add salt if necessary.

Cut the avocados into quarters, remove their skin and stones and crush with a fork, sprinkling them with lemon juice. Season with salt.

Wash the small courgette and grate it. Mix the courgette into the avocado purée.

To serve: arrange each of four plates as follows:
• a few essene biscuits (or an essene bread roll) and a spoonful of tapenade
• a dome of parsley tabbouleh
• a few spoonfuls grated courgette guacamole
• the tomato salad sprinkled with sprouted fennel shoots

Lettuce with lentil sprouts, walnut oil and turmeric

Sprouted green lentils have quite a strong flavour, so they are paired here with the milder, softer accents of avocado and served one spoonful per guest.

1 lettuce
1 avocado
4 or 5 heaped tablespoons green lentil sprouts

For the salad dressing:
5 tablespoons walnut oil
1 pinch turmeric
Salt

Put the nut oil with the turmeric in a salad bowl, and add salt.

Before you toss the salad, the lentils can be blanched as recommended (page 34).

Add the washed and drained lettuce leaves, the diced avocado and the lentil sprouts. Mix everything. Serve immediately.

Sprouts in main dishes

Two-lentil salad

The leftovers of cooked green lentils can be turned into a salad by mixing them into a creamy sauce using liquid oat cream (comes in a carton and is used a bit like liquid soya cream). Sprouted lentils add another dimension to a dish and make it crisp and healthy.

1 bowl cooked green lentils
150 ml liquid oat cream
2 tablespoons sesame oil
Salt
1 pinch curry powder

5 heaped tablespoons sprouted lentils

Place the sprouted lentils in the steamer basket and soften them just for a few seconds by steaming or boiling them in a pan of water.

Make the sauce in a salad bowl: mix the sesame oil with the curry and salt. Stir in the liquid oat cream. Mix well with the cooked green lentils. Sprinkle the salad with sprouted lentils. Serve immediately.

Warm salad of sprouted chick peas and chard with ume vinaigrette

Ume juice is a condiment that can be used like vinegar. It is a slightly acid juice made from Japanese umeboshi plums. It smells of flowers with a hint of cherry. This chard salad is served warm to bring out the aromas of the dressing and soften the chick peas.

A dozen chard leaves
1 bowl chick pea sprouts

For the ume vinaigrette:
2 tablespoons ume juice
6 tablespoons sunflower or sesame oil

Prepare the chick peas as on page 22 after 3 days' germination.

Wash and cut the chard leaves into strips with scissors. Put them together with the chick pea sprouts in the basket of a heavy-bottomed casserole and steam over a low heat for 10 to 15 minutes.

Pour the ume juice into a salad bowl and mix in the spoonfuls of oil one at a time. This dressing does not need seasoning, just a tiny pinch of salt according to taste.

Add the chard and chick pea sprouts, stir and serve immediately.

Fennel Terrine

A light vegetable custard that brings out the flavour of the fennel in two ways, as a bulb and as little shoots.

2 fennel bulbs
1 carrot
$^{1}/_{2}$ glass water
3 eggs
$^{1}/_{2}$ glass rice milk
1 teaspoon caraway seeds
4 tablespoons sprouted fennel seed shoots
2 tablespoons olive oil
Salt

Slice the fennel and carrot into discs. Cook in a heavy-bottomed casserole with the lid on in a little water (the glass you use for measuring should hold 150 ml). Salt lightly.

When the vegetables are cooked, put the cooking juices aside. Blend to a purée adding the rice milk. Leave to cool slightly before adding the eggs. Blend again.

Preheat the oven to Mark 7/220°C.

Oil a loaf tin and scatter caraway seeds over the bottom. Pour in the vegetable mixture and put in the oven for 25 minutes.

Put the olive oil in a small bowl, add the cooking juices and adjust the seasoning. Add the fennel shoots.

Serve the terrine hot and season it with the dressing.

If you serve it cold, it will be easier to cut into slices to serve as a first course.

Gourmet omelette

You can replace the thick soya cream with the liquid sort or with dairy-free milk (soya, rice, etc) to give the omelette a different, less firm consistency.

For 2 people:
3 eggs
3 heaped tablespoons thick soya cream
Herb salt
2 tablespoons wheat or sunflower sprouts
3 tablespoons sprouted alfalfa shoots

Beat the eggs with a fork together with the thick soya cream. Season with salt and pour into a hot, oiled frying pan. Cover.

When the omelette starts to form, scatter the wheat sprouts over it and stir them into the surface mixture with a fork.

Keep the heat low. Off the heat, scatter alfalfa shoots on the omelette and serve immediately.

Creamy sunflower risotto

In this recipe, the sunflower sprouts are added after the rice is cooked. A comforting dish to put with sautéed vegetables with mushrooms or courgettes and other steamed vegetables.

2 glasses brown round rice (240 g)
4 glasses water (600 ml)

2 heaped tablespoons blanched almond purée
2 glasses water (300 ml)
Salt, pepper, nutmeg
3 tablespoons sprouted sunflower seeds

Put the rice and water into a casserole dish. Place over a very low heat and put the lid on.

Add the water to the almond purée. You can put the mixture in a jar with a lid, then shake vigorously to obtain a creamy milk.

When the rice water is completely absorbed, pour in the almond milk. Cover and leave the rice to swell for 5 minutes off the heat.

Just before serving the risotto, put the casserole on a low heat and stir to stop it sticking, season with salt, pepper and nutmeg and add the sunflower seed sprouts.

Serve piping hot.

Paella of rice and sprouts

This dish of rice with vegetables is enriched after cooking by the addition of a mix of sprouts. I often use red lentils to balance this dish and add colour, but you can just as well use other sprouts instead.

2 glasses brown Thai rice (240 g)
4 glasses water (600 ml)
1 red pepper
1 fennel bulb
1 tablespoon mixed spice for paella (usually contains mild smoked paprika, rosemary and saffron)
1 shallot
4 tablespoons olive oil
3 tablespoons sprouted red lentils
2 tablespoons sprouted wheat

Cut the pepper, fennel bulb and shallot into strips, brown them in the olive oil and add the spice. Add the rice and stir. Cover with water, season with salt and leave to simmer with the lid on for 20 minutes over a low heat.

When the rice has absorbed all the stock, remove from the heat, sprinkle over the sprouts and leave to swell for 5 minutes with the lid on.

Vegetarian burgers

These are like vegetarian scallops. You can vary the recipe by adding grated vegetables or by adding garden herbs. The sprouted wheat has a sweetish flavour that compensates for the slight bitterness of the buckwheat in the flour.

1 glass buckwheat flour
2 glasses water (300 ml)
1 glass sprouted wheat or spelt
2 shallots
1 small carrot
A few parsley leaves
2 pinches salt

Add the water to the buckwheat flour, season with salt and add the sprouted wheat.

Grate the shallots and carrot and stir them into the batter.

Place a well oiled frying pan over a low heat. When the oil is hot, drop in a ladle of dough. Make 2 or 3 pancakes in this way. Put the lid on.

When the first side is cooked and a pale golden colour, turn the burgers over.

Serve piping hot with vegetables.

Quinoa and leek sprout burgers

The shoots of leeks, onions and radishes have a keen flavour and can sometimes be added to mixtures of flakes and grains to make vegetarian burgers. A sort of substitute for herbs.

8 tablespoons ready cooked quinoa
4 tablespoons chick pea flakes
4 tablespoons rice milk
6 button mushrooms
1 shallot
2 eggs
4 tablespoons leek seed sprouts

Put the chick pea flakes in a salad bowl and soak in the rice milk.

Peel and finely chop the shallot and mushrooms.

Mix the quinoa in with the chick pea flakes and add the eggs, mushrooms, shallot and leek shoots. Season with salt.

Place an oiled frying pan over a low heat. When it is hot, pour in the mixture. Put the lid on. After 5 to 10 minutes when the first side is cooked and the pancake quite firm, cut it into four using a spatula to make easier portions for turning over, then cook the other side.

Stuffed Pancakes

There are mixes of sprouted seed like radishes, mustard and alfalfa that are ideal for stuffing pancakes. You will also find ready packaged mixtures, including fennel and alfalfa.

For about ten pancakes:
200 g buckwheat flour
500 to 600 ml soya milk

Filling:
3 carrots
1 courgette or 1 leek
1 white onion
4 tablespoons olive oil
4 tablespoons alfalfa shoots
3 tablespoons sprouted radish seed shoots (or leek, or fenugreek)

Add the soya milk to the flour. This batter can be made in advance, but if it has thickened up, thin it with a little more dairy-free milk. You don't have to leave it to prove.

For the filling: Put the vegetables in a food processor and chop finely (you can also grate them). Soften gently in a frying pan over a low heat with olive oil. You can cook them with the lid on. Season with salt.

Make the pancakes in a very hot, oiled frying pan, spreading the batter with a spatula.

Fill each one with the vegetable mixture, add a few pinches of alfalfa, radish or leek shoots and fold the pancake over. Serve immediately.

Tabbouleh of aubergine salad

As in traditional tabbouleh recipes, this salad of sprouted wheat involves plenty of parsley. The aubergines are flavoured with cumin and cooked in oil with the lid on to give the dish a softer texture.

2 aubergines
1 teaspoon ground cumin
5 to 6 tablespoons olive oil
1 white onion
1 bunch flat leaf parsley
8 heaped tablespoons sprouted wheat (or spelt)
Salt

Peel the aubergines and dice finely.

Put the olive oil in a frying pan and brown the aubergines with a sprinkle of cumin and salt. Cover for a few moments until the pieces are tender.

Put the chopped parsley in a salad bowl together with the onion which has first been peeled and finely sliced. Add the sprouted wheat and the warm, cooked aubergines. Season with a little salt if necessary.

Stir everything thoroughly to bring out the aromas. Leave to cool.

Ratatouille and sprouted wheat

This ratatouille with olives is enhanced at the end of the cooking stage by the addition of sprouted wheat. It can be served hot or cold in summer dishes. The spelt can be replaced by wheat.

2 aubergines
3 courgettes
1 red pepper
2 garlic cloves
5 tablespoons olive oil
1 bay leaf
A dozen black olives
6 tablespoons sprouted wheat

Peel the aubergines and cut them into small cubes.

Slice the red pepper finely. Dice the courgette.

Pour the olive oil into a heavy-bottomed casserole and add the crushed garlic and aubergine cubes. Mix, then add the courgettes, the red pepper and the bay leaf.

Cook with the lid on over a low heat for about 25 minutes. When the vegetables start to soften, add the olives and the sprouted wheat. Season with salt and remove from the heat.

Vegetable purée with sprouted shoots

Vegetable purées always look more appetizing when decorated with green shoots. You can use this purée with a tofu sauté with cashew nuts, or a carrot curry with tempeh, etc.

2 courgettes
4 potatoes
2 tablespoons blanched almond purée
Salt
4 tablespoons sprouted garden cress shoots (or alfalfa)

Peel the potatoes and cut potatoes and courgettes into small pieces. Make the potato pieces smaller than the courgettes to balance the cooking time.

Put the vegetables in a heavy-bottomed casserole and just cover with water. Leave to cook for about 25 minutes over a low heat.

Put through a vegetable mill, adding a little cooking broth to obtain the desired consistency. Season with salt and mix in the almond purée, which should be liquid so that it melts easily. If this is not the case, dilute it beforehand with a few spoonfuls of the hot stock.

Serve with a sprinkling of garden cress or alfalfa shoots.

French bean casserole

Leek seed shoots have quite a strong flavour, and cooking them briefly with soy sauce will soften them and help to flavour the vegetables.

You can use onion seed shoots instead and proceed in the same way.

500 g French beans
1 cucumber
1 courgette
3 tablespoons leek seed shoots
2 tablespoons tamari (soy sauce)
2 tablespoons white sesame

Remove the strings from the beans and cut them into 3 or 4 cm long chunks. Cut the courgette and cucumber into broad disks. Steam the vegetables putting the French beans in first (5 minutes before the courgettes and cucumber).

Pour the soy sauce into a frying pan, add the leek shoots, stir quickly over a high heat and add the cooked French beans, courgette and cucumber. For a pretty contrast with the green vegetables, scatter them with white sesame seeds (unlike whole sesame, these are hulled).

Serve immediately.

Sautéed potatoes with onion shoots

The new potatoes are first steamed to make the sauté light, crispy and golden and low-fat. The onion shoots add a fresh, tender piquancy to this spring dish.

1 kg small new potatoes
3 or 4 tablespoons onion shoots
Dairy-free margarine or olive oil
Herb salt

Choose small new potatoes. Wash them, then steam.

Put two knobs of dairy-free margarine or three tablespoons olive oil in a large frying pan. Tip the cooked potatoes in, mix and season with herb salt.

Leave the potatoes to brown and add the onion shoots at the last minute. Serve immediately.

Sprouts and 'cheese'

Fresh sprout cheese

A substitute for garlic and chives. In dairy-free cheeses or goat's cheeses, you can use shoots as herbs or spices. An unusual way of seasoning and pairing flavours.

1 fresh goat's cheese (or 1 dairy-free soya-based cheese)
1 tablespoon sprouted alfalfa shoots (or radish, mustard or onion)
1 tablespoon chopped hazelnuts

Spread the chopped hazelnuts on a plate, lay the goat's cheese on them and roll it around so that the nuts stick to the sides. Top with shoots.

The hazelnuts are an optional addition, but I have found it interesting to marry the crunchy nuts with the smooth, creamy cheese and the fresh flavour of the leafy sprouts.

Alfalfa adds a delicate flavour but you can choose more piquant accents by using radish shoots: it depends on your taste!

Tofu cubes with sesame

Tofu is also called 'soya cheese'. When it is plain, it is a bit tasteless. But once it is seasoned and flavoured with sprouted seeds, it can be turned into astonishingly tasty mouthfuls to serve as an appetizer or on a cheese platter.

To add an extra dimension to the sprouted sesame, I have used gomasio, a mix of toasted sesame crushed with salt.

For a block of 100 g plain tofu:
1 teaspoon poppy seeds
3 tablespoons sprouted sesame seed
1 tablespoon gomasio

Cut the tofu into cubes with one and a half centimetre sides.

Mix together the gomasio and sprouted sesame (rinsed and drained) on a flat plate. Place the tofu cubes on the plate making the sesame mixture stick to the moist sides.

Arrange the tofu cubes on a large plate to create contrasting colours, scatter a few poppy seeds over them and put a cocktail stick in each.

Cream of soya

Thick soya cream has a smooth, rich consistency and can be seasoned to make a fresh dairy-free 'cheese'. With the spicy flavours of the sprouts of your choosing, it makes a perfect spread or dip for vegetables.

235 g pot thick soya cream
3 tablespoons sprouted alfalfa shoots (or mustard or garden cress)
Herb salt
2 tablespoons walnut, hazelnut or sesame oil

Put the oil and two pinches of salt in a bowl, add the thick soya cream and stir vigorously to a homogenous consistency.

Add the alfalfa and serve immediately.

It is often better not to add pepper to these spreads if you want to bring out the flavour of the shoots and discover their spicy character.

Upside-down green shoots and cheese

The sprouted shoots on these spreads are raw but also sealed under the melted cheese. This brings out their aromas in different ways according to whether you use the shoots of sprouted onion seed, rocket or leek, for example.

For 2 slices of bread:
2 large slices of spelt bread
1 goat's cheese
3 heaped tablespoons sprouted onion (or leek) seed shoots

Arrange half the shoots on the slices of bread. Spread slices of cheese over them. Put them under the grill for a few minutes.

When the cheese has melted, serve immediately and decorate with the rest of the shoots.

Fromage frais with shoots

A simple soya yogurt with a fine vegetable oil can be served as a salad dressing or as a fromage frais with a few raw vegetables.

For 1 plain soya yogurt:
1 tablespoon sprouted fennel seed shoots
2 tablespoons safflower oil
Salt

Or

For 1 plain soya yogurt:
1 tablespoon sprouted radish seed shoots
2 tablespoons rape seed oil
Salt

Mix the oil, pinch of salt and the yogurt to a smooth cream. Pour into little ramekins and sprinkle with fennel or radish shoots.

Arrange a ramekin on each plate with a choice of crudités around it.

Smoked tofu sandwich

Leafy sprouts and shoots pleasantly complement, and can even replace, salad in a sandwich. And they taste wonderfully healthy with a nutritional value that will pep up a meal eaten on the run.

For the dressing:
See the recipe for Cream of soya, page 98, using sprouted mustard seed shoots

Slices of spelt bread
200 g smoked tofu
1 cucumber
6 tablespoons sunflower seed shoots
A few round lettuce leaves

Half peel the cucumber. Slice it into very fine discs using a mandoline. Cut the block of smoked tofu into thin slices half a centimetre thick.

Fill the sandwiches with a layer of cucumber, spread with the sprouted mustard shoot dressing, lay two lettuce leaves over them, scatter the sunflower seed shoots on top and finally lay the slices of smoked tofu over everything.

Sprouts with desserts and fruit

Pear compote and sprouted wheat

Wheat sprouts have a naturally sweet flavour that makes them ideal as an accompaniment to desserts and snacks.

8 pears
5 tablespoons wheat or spelt sprouts

Cut the fruit into quarters and put them in a heavy-bottomed casserole. Cover and cook over a very low heat for 25 minutes. Blend (or not, according to taste) and leave to cool.

Mix the sprouted wheat with the stewed fruit and serve in dessert bowls.

Stewed apples stuffed with sprouted sesame

Depending on the variety you use, the apples can also be baked in the oven with the lid on. Reine de Reinettes or other pippin-type dessert apples are particularly suited to this method.

5 apples
10 dried apricots
5 tablespoons honey
6 tablespoons sprouted sesame
2 pinches ground cinnamon

Core the apples and stuff each one with two dried apricots. Place them in a heavy-bottomed casserole with a few spoonfuls of water. Cover and leave to cook over a very low heat for 20 to 30 minutes.

Mix the honey, cinnamon and sprouted sesame. When the apples are cooked, arrange them in each dish pouring a spoonful of the sesame-honey mixture over the apricots. Serve warm.

Dates stuffed with... dates

These make very healthy sweets that are packed full of energy and easy to take on a picnic or outing. Fresh Medjool dates are particularly excellent for their soft, fleshy consistency.

A dozen fresh dates

For the stuffing:
5 to 6 tablespoons sprouted sunflower seeds
3 tablespoons sprouted whole sesame
6 to 8 dates

Agave syrup

Make the stuffing in the blender: put the rinsed and drained sprouts in the bowl with the dates. Blend to a paste.

Using a knife, split all the other dates and take out the stones. Stuff each date with a knob of the sprout paste.

If you are making a plate of these sweets for festive meals, you can make the stuffed dates glisten by applying a little agave syrup with the back of a spoon. You can use honey instead of agave syrup but this will be sweeter.

Pine kernel and sunflower sprout mousse

This is a surprising dish made with agar-agar jelly. When it is firm, it is blended with the sprouts and turns into a frothy relish. This light mousse is not too sweet and can be served with cake or used as a substitute for custard. On its own as a dessert, it is tastier when served with this mix of kernels and rice syrup.

1 litre almond-hazelnut dairy-free milk
4 g powdered agar-agar
8 to 10 tablespoons sprouted sunflower seeds
6 tablespoons pine kernels
4 to 6 tablespoons rice syrup

Put the agar-agar in a casserole dish with the dairy-free milk. Place over a low heat, stirring frequently. When the mixture starts to simmer, give it 3 minutes, then pour it into a salad bowl.

Leave to cool in the fridge for about 2 hours until the custard is completely jellified.

Brown the kernels in a dry frying pan.

Tip the sprouted sunflower seeds into the liquidizer goblet and add the custard. Blend long enough to obtain a frothy emulsion and a really creamy consistency. Pour into dessert bowls and put in the fridge for 30 minutes, which is the length of time it takes for the cream to become aerated and mousse-like. Pour into dessert bowls, scatter with the browned kernels and pour over the rice syrup.

Dairy-free milkshake with sprouts

Drinks can be made by crushing the sprouts in a little water then diluting. However by replacing the water with ready-made dairy-free milk you get a flavour that is easier to acquire.

My favourite is rice milk, which is naturally sweet and makes an ideal pairing with certain seeds. Other dairy-free milks include almond, hazelnut, quinoa and spelt, which you can put according to taste with 'sweet' sprouted seed (wheat, spelt, sunflower, etc) to give them a slightly sweet flavour.

You should use one glass of dairy-free milk to about 2 tablespoons sprouts. In general, it is not necessary to sweeten the mixture as it is sufficiently tasty without the addition of sugar. But it you prefer, choose a liquid sugar like agave syrup or liquid grain syrup, which melt easily in a milkshake.

Start by putting the dairy-free milk in the fridge to obtain a chilled non-iced drink.

Blend rice milk with a few pinches sunflower seed sprouts.

Blend oat milk with a few pinches wheat or spelt sprouts.

Blend spelt milk with a few pinches spelt sprouts.

Melon salad

Ripe yellow melons are often very sweet. Their soft white flesh goes surprisingly well with the aniseed flavour of fennel shoots. A combination to enhance a dessert buffet and delight your guests.

1 yellow melon (about 800 g)
5 to 6 tablespoons sprouted fennel seed shoots

Peel the melon and remove the seeds. Cut cubes into a salad bowl and scatter with fennel seed shoots.

Dairy-free yogurt

For breakfast or at tea-time, this makes an ideal energy-booster.

If you have it as a dessert, you can replace the yogurt with soya fromage blanc with a drizzle of agave syrup whipped in.

For 1 soya yogurt:
1 tablespoon raisins
2 tablespoons sprouted alfalfa shoots

The day or a few hours before, soak the raisins in a glass of water. Drain before mixing with dairy-free yogurt. Sprinkle with alfalfa.

Banana cream for breakfast

This cream is quick to prepare and leaves you time to savour its simple flavours. So take a moment to appreciate the sweetness of the banana, the rich creamy texture and the tender sunflower seeds.

For 1 banana:
4 to 5 tablespoons soya fromage blanc
3 to 4 tablespoons sprouted sunflower seeds

Peel and crush the banana then stir in the dairy-free fromage blanc to obtain a cream. Scatter with sprouted sunflower seeds. Serve immediately.

Grass juices

Healthy Gazpacho

There are no tomatoes in this unusual gazpacho where green has pride of place. I suggest lightly steaming the vegetables to soften them. The soup will then be easier to blend to a smooth consistency.

2 young courgettes
2 cucumbers
1 garlic clove
1 small white onion
3 tablespoons powdered barley grass juice

Peel the cucumber and cut the cucumber and courgettes into small pieces. Put them in the steamer basket and steam for a brief 5 minutes with the peeled garlic and onion.

Tip all the vegetables into the liquidizer goblet, add the powdered barley juice, cover with cold water and blend.

Add a pinch of salt and enough cold water to obtain a soup consistency. Pour into small bowls.

Barley grass vinaigrette

A dressing to drizzle over crudités or the white part of steamed leeks, or for coating a salad of green beans or grated courgettes.

1 teaspoon powdered barley juice
1 teaspoon water
4 teaspoons cold pressed rape seed oil
Herb salt

Reconstitute the powdered barley juice with water and emulsify by adding the oil. Salt lightly.

Last minute warm broth

Quick and easy to make, this clear broth gets its flavour from the soy sauce, while the barley juice gives it the flavour of green vegetables. I preferred not to cook the barley juice and use water that is just simmering.

Basis for 1 person:
150 ml water
1 tablespoon tamari (soy sauce)
1 tablespoon powdered barley grass juice

Heat the water.

Pour the soy sauce into a cup or glass. Add the powdered barley grass juice.

When the water starts to bubble, pour it into the glass. Stir and drink immediately. It tastes excellent!

Celeriac purée

This light purée makes an excellent accompaniment to sautéed tofu with herbs or grain or vegetable croquettes. Celeriac has a discreet flavour that goes well with barley juice while also turning it a pretty pale green colour. The walnut oil can be replaced by an excellent virgin grapeseed oil (an unrefined and non-deodorised organic oil with a clean fragrance).

1 or 2 celeriac (800 g)
1 slice lemon
1 tablespoon powdered barley grass juice
Herb salt
2 to 3 tablespoons walnut oil (or olive oil)

Peel the celeriac and slice. Put the slices in a heavy-bottomed casserole with just enough water to cover them. Squeeze the juice of the lemon slice and add to the water so that the celeriac keeps its white colour.

Cook over a low heat for 15 minutes.

Reconstitute the powdered barley juice with four or five tablespoons water, adding them one at a time.

When the celeriac pieces are soft, put them in the liquidizer or through the vegetable mill. To obtain the purée consistency, add some of the cooking stock. Season with salt and add the oil and barley juice.

ACONBURY SPROUTS LIMITED

Unit 4 Westwood Industrial Estate, Pontrilas, Hereford HR2 0EL

Tel: 01981 241155 Fax: 01981 241386
Email: info@aconbury.co.uk www.aconbury.co.uk

Suppliers of fresh organic bean sprouts, sprouted seeds and wheatgrass.
For more information on their wheatgrass:
www.wheatgrass-uk.com or ring the dedicated wheatgrass line on 01981 241336.

UK JUICERS LIMITED

Unit 5 Harrier Court, Airfield Business Park, Elvington, York YO41 4EA

Tel: 01904 757070 Fax: 01904 757071
Email: enquiries@ukjuicers.com www.ukjuicers.com

Specialists in high quality masticating juicers, citrus and wheatgrass juicers, water purifiers, books and other health products.

WHOLISTIC RESEARCH COMPANY LIMITED

Unit 1, Five House Farm, Sandon Road, Therfield, Royston, Herts, SG8 9RE

Tel: 08454 303100 Fax: 08454 303200
Email: info@wholisticresearch.com www.wholistichealthdirect.co.uk

Suppliers of products that help achieve maximum health and vitality, including juicers, sprouters, seeds for sprouting and books.

Index of Recipes